SCHIRMER'S LIBRARY OF MUSICAL CLASSICS

Vol. 2028

Franz Liszt

Keyboard Essentials

For Piano

ISBN 0-7935-6127-2

G. SCHIRMER, Inc.

DISTRIBUTED BY

HAL•LEONARD®
CORPORATION
7777 W. BLUEMOUND RD. P.O. BOX 13819 MILWAUKEE, WI 53213

FOREWORD

Franz Liszt, the incomparable, transcendental virtuoso pianist; the visionary composer; the very personification of the 19th-century Romantic artist-hero: certainly these are common images—somewhat truthful images—of this often misunderstood larger-than-life musician. But there are other facets to Liszt's piano music. He was also the composer of small, often intimate pieces of moderate difficulty, of exquisite sacred miniatures, of settings of his native Hungarian folk music, of charming album leaves, of pieces for children, as well as experimental musical excursions decades ahead of his time.

The present volume presents a comprehensive collection of these smaller, eminently playable and approachable pieces for the pianist of moderate technical skill, as well as for the student or amateur interested in tracing the lifelong stylistic development of the composer. Here there is no *Liebestraum*, no *Mephisto Waltz* or *B-Minor Sonata*, and certainly none of the intimidating opera paraphrases or Bach transcriptions. And yet—as if perfectly distilled—the entire range of Liszt's compositional style is present and uncompromised, from the lyricism of *En Rêve* and *Consolation No. 1* through the *Five Hungarian Folksongs* and various sacred pieces, on to the strikingly iconoclastic territory of *Nuages Gris* and *La Lugubre Gondola*.

Born during Beethoven's middle period and still composing after the births of Schoenberg, Bartók and Stravinsky, Liszt more than any other composer both opened and closed a musical era. The works in this volume, spanning his long career, provide a technical and musical introduction to his piano writing as well as a fascinating survey of his development as a composer.

WALTZ IN A MAJOR

Franz Liszt

(Moderato ♩ = ca. 144)

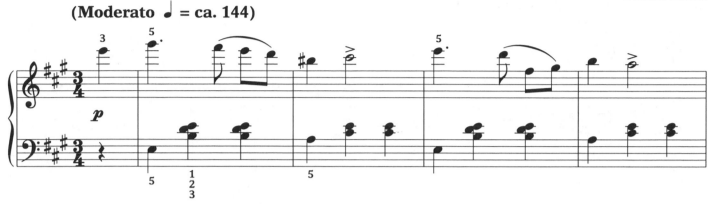

ALBUM LEAF IN WALTZ FORM
Simplified Transcription

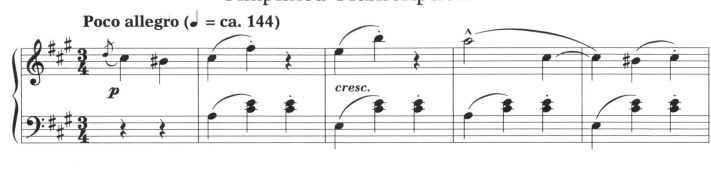

MADAME PELET-NARBONNE'S
MERRY-GO-ROUND

Allegro intrepido

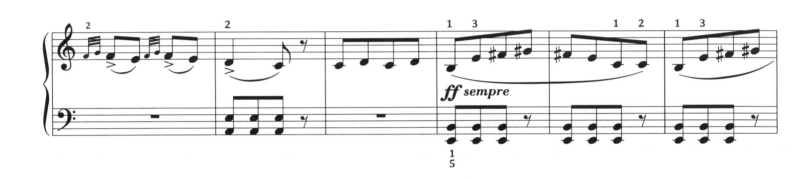

Un poco moderato

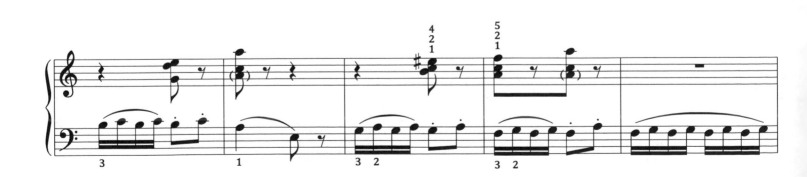

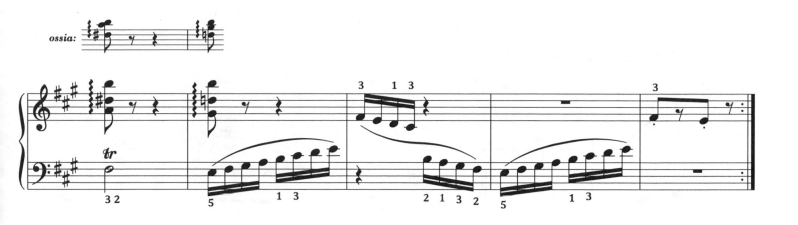

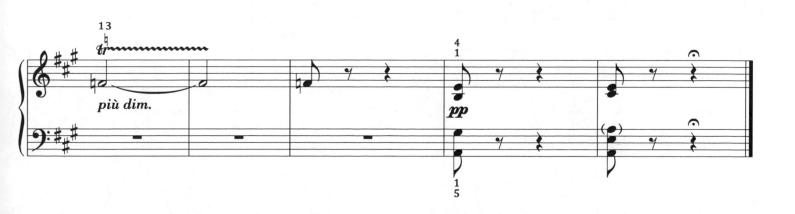

CHRISTMAS SONG
Christ is Born

a) smaller hands: b)

LA CLOCHE SONNE
(The Ringing Bell)

This arrangement of an old French song, dating from about 1850, is now published for the first time. It is written on one side of a MS. sheet. On another sheet Liszt has written out the vocal outline and words of the original song.

In this edition, all dynamic, phrasing and other interpretative indications have been added by the Editor. The autograph MS., in the Liszt Museum, Weimar, is entirely unmarked.

I am indebted to the Director of the Liszt Museum, Weimar, for so kindly placing the material at my disposal.

edited by Jack Werner

AVE MARIA

This hitherto-unpublished 'Ave Maria' is Liszt's own arrangement for piano solo of his fourth setting of the Latin hymn for voice and piano (or harmonium). The autograph MS, in the Hungarian National Museum, Budapest, is signed '28ten Mai, '81, F.L.', that is ten days later than the 'Wiegenlied'.

The arrangement follows fairly closely the opening and concluding phrases of the song version. The words of the latter, which consists of 32 bars, are: 'Ave Maria, Dominum tecum benedicta tu in mulieribus et benedictus. Ave Maria.'

Liszt edited the work with evident care, providing most of the phrasing and dynamic indications. He also inserted a few pedal marks and added fingering for one passage, as shown.

I am indebted to the Director of the Hungarian National Museum, Budapest, for so kindly placing the material at my disposal.

edited by Jack Werner

✦ The fingering of this passage is Liszt's own.

to A. Siloti

ABSCHIED*
(Farewell)

*Russian folk song

NUAGES GRIS
(Gray Clouds)

WIEGENLIED
(Cradle Song)

This poetic and evocative 'Wiegenlied', now published for the first time, was composed in 1881, five years before Liszt's death. It was written for Arthur Friedheim, one of Liszt's best pupils, who also acted as his private secretary for a time, and bears the following inscription:

'An Arthur Friedheim,

(Weimar)   18ten Mai, '81,

freundlichst

andenken,

F. Liszt.

'To Arthur Friedheim, (Weimar), 18th May, in friendliest remembrance, F. Liszt.'

Arthur Friedheim, later a well-known pianist, was born in St. Petersburg in 1859. After teaching in Leipzig and at the Manchester Royal College of Music, he settled in New York, where he died in 1932.

Though only the first four bars of the right hand are phrased in the original MS. (in the Nationalbibliothek, Vienna), Liszt has paid particular attention throughout to pedalling, as well as inserting fingering in a number of places. In this edition I have provided further phrasing, fingering and dynamic indications.

I am indebted to the Director of the Vienna Nationalbibliothek for so kindly placing the material at my disposal.

edited by Jack Werner

ALBUM LEAF IN WALTZ FORM

O HEILIGE NACHT!
(O Holy Night)

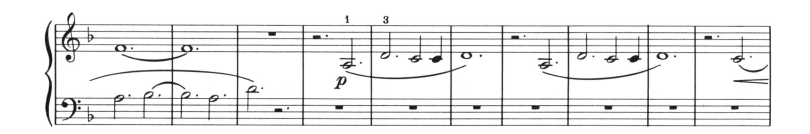

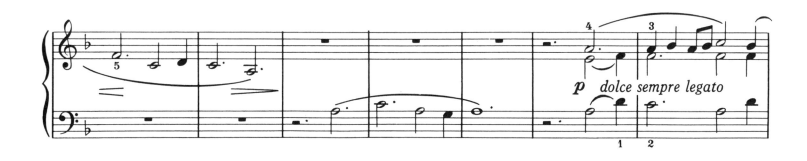

FOUR LITTLE PIANO PIECES

1

(1865)

2

(1865)

3

(1873)

4

(1876)

LÄNDLER IN A-FLAT MAJOR

This Chopinesque little Waltz was written in the autograph album of Princess Amalie von Donaueschingen in 1843, when Liszt was 32 years of age. Headed simply 'Ländler', with no tempo indication, and signed 'F. Liszt, Donau Eschingen, 25 Nov. 1843', it is written on two facing pages, each decorated with a pretty floral border typical of the musical autograph albums of the period.

The composition remained unknown until 1921, when it was printed for the first time in a Stuttgart music magazine. It has not reappeared since.

The present edition has been prepared from the original MS. since the Stuttgart version contains a number of errors. Phrasing and dynamics have been provided, as well as fingering and pedalling.

The original autograph MS. is in the Fürstl. Fürstenbergische Hofbibliothek, Donaueschingen, to the Director of which I am indebted for so kindly placing the material at my disposal.

edited by Jack Werner

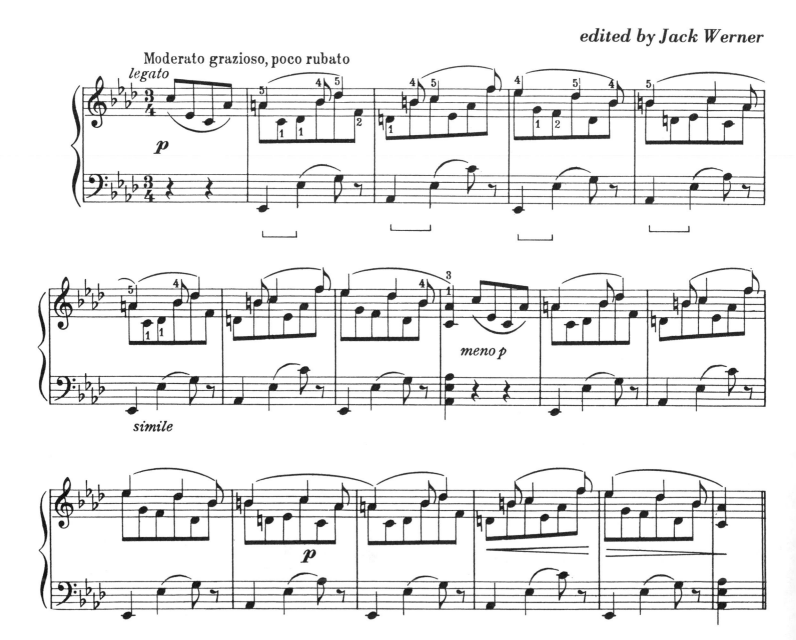

ABENDGLOCKEN
(Evening Bells)

CONSOLATIONS NO. 1

edited by *Rafael Joseffy*

ALBUM LEAF

to my young friend August Stradal

EN REVE
(Dreaming)
Nocturne

PIANO PIECE IN A-FLAT MAJOR NO. 2

Andantino espressivo

FIVE HUNGARIAN FOLKSONGS*

1

edited by Joseph Prostakoff

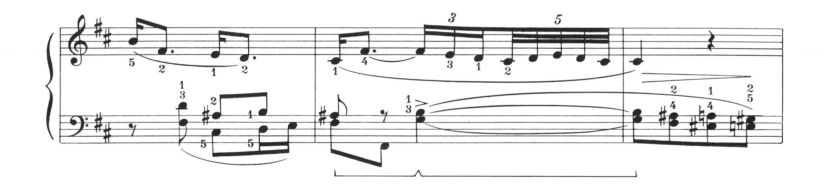

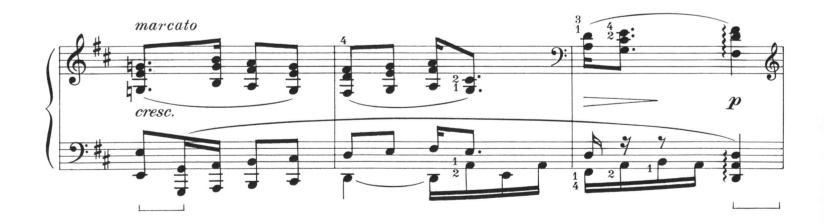

*Four of the pieces in this cycle are headed in the original by texts of Hungarian folksongs, to indicate the mood of the music. An English approximation is given.

2

If I had all the treasures of the ocean,
I would give them
If I could call you my wife.

Allegretto
con grazia

3

Oh, how sad is my life since you left me,
You were the star of my happiness.
The night is so dark without stars.

4

I looked everywhere but
I could not find a suitable horse.
So I stole the commissary's horse.

"I beg you, commissary,
Don't shoot my horse."
"You are so stupid that
You care more for your horse
Than for your life!"

5

In the deep forest a turtle-dove cries for his mate.
I am crying for my love.

EHEMALS
(Formerly)

TYROLEAN MELODY

This unknown 'Tyrolean Melody' by Liszt appeared in a volume of music published in Manchester about 1856. Entitled 'The Athenaeum Musicale', the volume consists of 'Songs and duets . . . with a choice selection of Foreign Marches, Waltzes, Polonoises (*sic*) . . . . selected from the works of Classical Composers for the Piano Forte including Mozart, Beethoven, Weber, Liszt, Thalberg and Mozart Junr., the latter being now published for the first time in England'.

The 'Tyrolean Melody' is described as 'Arranged by Francois Liszt', and there is a note to the effect that its inclusion in the volume is 'By Permission of Mrs. Chappell', who presumably owned the MS. I have failed to find any mention of this composition in any book of reference.

The few editorial indications of the original have been incorporated.

edited by Jack Werner

LA LUGUBRE GONDOLA I
(The Funeral Gondola I)

LA LUGUBRE GONDOLA II
(The Funeral Gondola II)